Memories of
St Budeaux

Memories of
St Budeaux
by
Derek Tait

Driftwood Coast Publishing

Frontispiece : Outside 11 Tamar Terrace, St Budeaux.

First published 2009

Driftwood Coast Publishing
PO Box 7,West Park,Plymouth,PL5 2YS.
© Derek Tait, 2009

ISBN number : 9780956078124
Price £9.99.

Contents

Acknowledgements

Photo credits : The Driftwood Coast Photo Library, Maurice Dart, Ray Rylatt, Helen Wyler, William Hutchinson, Ray McSweeney, Philip Syms and Jerry Richards.
Thanks also to all the people who have written to me over the years sending their memories and photos.
Thanks to all the people who have shared their memories for this book. These include Marshall Ware, Sally Ware, Maurice Dart, Ray Rylatt, G G Mitchell, Mrs W C Camp, George H Ivory, Helen Wyler, Walter Harris, Ray McSweeney, Mr L Tucker, Graham Sullivan, Pat Twyford and Philip Syms.
I have tried to track down the copyright owners of all photos used and apologise to anyone who hasn't been mentioned.
Check out my website at www.derektait.co.uk

Bibliography

Books:
Images of England : Plymouth by Derek Tait (Tempus 2003).
Plymouth at War by Derek Tait (Tempus 2006).
Saltash Passage by Derek Tait (Driftwood Coast 2007).
St Budeaux by Derek Tait (Driftwood Coast 2007).

Websites:
Brian Moseley's Plymouth Data website at: www.plymouthdata.info
Derek Tait's Plymouth Local History Blog at:
http://plymouthlocalhistory.blogspot.com/

Newspapers
The Evening Herald
The Western Independent
The Western Morning News
The Western Weekly Mercury

Driftwood Coast Publishing
© Derek Tait 2009

Introduction

I'm glad that many people enjoyed my book about St Budeaux and I was pleased that so many people wrote to me and shared their memories and photos. It made me realise that these personal memories capture what it was actually like to live in St Budeaux at the time and it seemed a shame that eventually a lot of these reminiscences would be forgotten and lost forever. I was lucky to have known the local historian, Marshall Ware, for many years and he told me some very interesting stories of days gone by and I've done my best to recall in this book as many as I can. Stories have also been drawn from Marshall's own papers and cuttings and I'm sure they will prove very interesting reading to many people. Marshall's own memories of St Budeaux went back a long way. Born in 1906, he saw many changes to the area over the years.

Included in this book are tales of nude bathing in the Tamar, Little Ash Tea Gardens, school days, the St Budeaux Regatta, the Second World War, transport and many quirky stories that people have recalled from the last hundred or so years.

Old newspapers are always a good source of long forgotten information. I've included stories and photos from papers dating back to 1909. It could be that these are the only copies in existence so the stories covered in them won't have been featured anywhere else. There are some very interesting photos from the St Budeaux Carnival of 1909 included.

St Budeaux has certainly changed a great deal in the last one hundred years. The days of the trams are now long gone and even many tourists visiting the area of Saltash Passage know little about the American soldiers leaving from there for D-Day, although, thankfully, many people do remember and there are regular memorial services held.

Gone too are many buildings though a lot still remain such as the 16th century barn off Normandy Hill, the Trelawny Inn, St Budeaux Church, the Royal Albert Bridge Inn, the Ferry House Inn and the Cornwall's Gate Inn (originally the vicarage). Many of the old terraced houses also remain such as the ones in St Budeaux Square. New housing estates have been built in the last 60 or so years changing the landscape completely in areas such as Barne Barton and Bull Point. The building of the Tamar Bridge and the Parkway, though now themselves a part of history, are a recent change to many people that have altered the landscape forever.

I hope that the few memories featured within the pages of this book will not only prove interesting reading but will also increase people's knowledge of the area.

St Budeaux Square, in the photo below, is still easily recognisable. The Trelawny Inn is on the left and still stands today. The awnings show where the shops of the day were. This picture was probably taken in the 1950s and although there are many people, there is little traffic. One solitary car is parked further down the road. Shops that can be recognised include Reid's and Maypole. There's an empty gap beside the Trelawny, now filled with Ivor Dewdney's shop selling pasties, and an old red telephone box stands there. Nearby there are Belisha beacons but no zebra crossing and on the pavement is an old red post box. The layout of the road has certainly changed over the years and it's incredible to think that the area was once so traffic free. The fashions have also seen some changes. The people in this photo are dressed in heavy dark coloured coats and many of the women are wearing hats.

Amongst cuttings and items belonging to Marshall Ware, I found the following interesting reminiscences of G G Mitchell regarding Barne Barton. These memories date back to a time long before the current estates were built and show life as it once was when St Budeaux was a lot quieter place.

G G Mitchell remembered:

I know of three wells at Barne Barton, one under the cellar of a small building at the left of the house, in the sheep's yard, which supplied the house with water. Another well in the Orchard, on the right hand side of the house, which had slabs of blue stone where we used to keep the cream during hot weather. There was also a very deep well half way up the hill in West Down. It had a little house built around it and a pump.

The name of the field in front of our house was Open Down and the two fields above were called Higher and Lower Gratton. The field overlooking Camel's Head was called One Tree Hill and the field near Meera was Morris Park.

On the right hand side of the farm, as you would enter the yard, there used to be a barn with a thrashing machine which would thrash the corn which would then be carried in sacks up the steps into the higher part of the barn. Afterwards, the corn would be crushed for cattle feed. The machinery in the barn was worked by two horses underneath who would walk round and round. The chickens, ducks and geese would have a fine time picking up the spilled grain.

We grew three fields of corn each year. My parents kept four men and a boy on the farm and two servants in the house. Three of the men's names were Doidge, Henwood and Ham. Hutchings was the name of the boy. I can't remember the name of the houseman and I do not know their Christian names. Doidge was an excellent man for growing vegetables and we had the contract to supply the RN Barracks with vegetables. A load, on a horse and wagon, would go there most mornings. Doidge would be up in the field cutting cabbage and cauliflower at 5 o'clock in the morning. We had a large walled garden which grew vegetables for the house and all fruit including William Pears and Victoria Plums trained against the high wall. Doidge also thatched all the corn ricks.

Ham was the cowman and before him, there was a man called Peard. We had 60 South Devon cows and supplied the Plymouth Co-op with milk. We also supplied J P Cundy and sold a lot of dairy produce at the door.

Henwood looked after the sheep and the hedges on the farm. The lambs grew so well on Barne and we could always supply the butchers with Easter lamb mainly Mr A Sleeman of William Street in Devonport.

We had a cow shed with 12 fat bullocks which were for the Christmas market and were mostly bought by the Plymouth Co-op. My father was a close friend of Mr Endacott who was head of the Co-op at that time.

The houseman did the ploughing and tillage. The farm and land around Bull Point was 220 acres. We had 7 horses and my pony. The Trelawny's were very good landlords and used to send a working bailiff and a gang of men from Coldrenick to do endless repairs to the farm and we had a bathroom and toilet upstairs in the house in 1914.
We used to get invited to wonderful garden parties at Coldrenick House.

It's hard to imagine that a lot of the area was once farm land with horses and cows. It's hard to imagine too that there were once orchards in the area. One can still be found today though, at the end of the Kloof in Saltash Passage, near to where the path joins Normandy Hill. Long since overgrown, it has been earmarked as a building plot for new houses. It's another development which, if it goes ahead, will change the landscape forever and the orchard will long be forgotten.

The Western Independent of 12th April 1953 recalled the first days of St Budeaux. A Mrs W C Camp recalled her memories of Millbrook Cottages at the time and of the people who lived nearby.

Mrs W C Camp remembered:
My family lived in the district and remembered the cottages being demolished about fifty years ago. They were the first houses to be built in the area and Victoria Road is located where they once stood. Further along the road was a farmhouse which was occupied by the late Mr and Mrs Westlake. Their daughter, a 79 year old Mrs C Harvey, now lives at 5 Tamar Terrace, Normandy Way and she can

remember the twenty-odd families who had their homes there. She used to go with her father to deliver the daily milk to the cottages. Mrs Harvey remembered the photographer, Mr Gilhen, who took the photo of Millbrook Cottages in 1893. She also had a photograph of her father delivering the milk taken at the same time. Mrs Harvey didn't remember when the cottages were built but they were there before her mother was born and may have even been erected before her grandparents time. She also recalled the Wesleyan Church which stood further down the road. It was originally an old stable.

From the previous photo, it's possible to imagine where the subsequent Victoria Road was built. Many people driving or walking along this section of Victoria Road won't realise that these little cottages once stood in its place.

On 11th April, 1954, the Western Independent featured an article about George H Ivory and a talk he gave to the St Budeaux Baptist Church Men's Fellowship. Mr Ivory recalled events from his childhood which dated back to 1892.

George H Ivory remembered:
My father was in the Army and he travelled a good deal in the first few years of his life. While he was still a child, the family returned to England to settle down at St Budeaux. It was probably because this was my first taste of English life that it remains so clearly in my memory. In those days, Plympton was part of the Plympton Rural

District. Except for farming, the nearest place for industry was the Naval Depot at Bull Point. There was also an Artillery Barracks, a Metropolitan Police Depot and quarters for officers and workmen. There was a day school and a Sunday school at Bull Point of which the headmistress was Miss Cross, who later married Mr Touranac, a Devonport saddler.

Kinterbury Road, leading from Bull Point to St Budeaux, ran through Barne Barton Farm which was occupied by Mr and Mrs Joe Cuddiford. Their sons, Edward and Joseph, and daughters, Mary and Maggie, died long ago. There was one pond in the farmstead and another below the hollow in Kinterbury Road where the boys used to catch minnows and tadpoles. In the Winter, it sometimes froze over and was used as a skating rink.

Saltash Passage consisted of two dozen houses. The Royal Albert Bridge had then been built only thirty three years. The Ferry Inn was occupied by Mr Wiles who played the violin and used to take part in local concerts with his daughter, who played the piano. A wayside chapel, St Peter's, had been built seven years before as a memorial to an Admiral. Mr Norman's daughters kept the little shop near the ferry and Mr Batters used to hire rowing boats with leg-of-mutton sails.

On the road from the Passage to lower St Budeaux, on the left side, there were two short rows of pink cottages belonging to the L and SW Railway. The station was only a year old, as was the Trelawny Hotel, whose first occupant, a Mr Stripling, died a year later when the lease was taken by Mr Hearn. The village shop, owned by Mrs Eastlike, was in Yeoman Terrace. Another of the four houses were occupied by two old maiden ladies, the Misses Henley and West, who kept school. Grannie Rowe's Cottage was at the foot of Barn Lane near the station.

The St Budeaux 'big house' was Mount Tamar in Kings Tamerton, which was occupied by Colonel Chard VC of Rorke's Drift fame. There were two farms worked by the Bradford and Cole families. Mr George Cole was the church organist.

At the top of St Budeaux hill were the first seven houses of Clifford Terrace. Two of the occupants were Mr Bonney and Mr Mortimer, who both had long white beards. Further on was the school with 'Skipper' Warring as headmaster. The boys in this section of the parish were hostile to those from the lower areas and it was awkward to go to, or leave, the church on Sundays, for it was not unusual to be stoned. The same treatment was meted out when one crossed the ferry into Saltash.

Honicknowle was further east, whilst Knackersknowle (later

Crownhill), though in the same parish, was almost foreign country. One remarkable character was a bearded giant from Honicknowle called Rowe, who had a cart with four donkeys harnessed in line to pull it. When the spirit moved him, he would stop his caravan, stand up on his load, and preach the gospel. He had a large family of fine sons. There were no resident doctors and no health services. Night soil was buried in the back garden. Water was hand-pumped from the well in each garden. There was no gas nor electric light, no health insurance, no unemployed, no buses, no trams, no automobiles, no aeroplanes, no wireless and no cinema. The only two great inventions in the countryside, in those days, were the railways and the telegraph - when they were available.
A steam roller was a rare and wonderful sight. A man had to walk ahead of it with a red flag. Horses would shy and bolt if not carefully led past. Our butcher was Mr Robertshaw from Ford who called twice a week. Bread and cakes were made at home in the kitchen. In spite of all our limitations, we seemed a very healthy community with plenty of resource and a great respect for our neighbours. People seemed more distinguished than nowadays.

This view of the Royal Albert Bridge shows children in Victorian times paddling and taking a dip in the waters of the Tamar. It's hard to imagine a similar occurrence today especially with the river's muddy banks littered with sharp rocks and various broken bottles. In the background is the training ship for wayward boys, the T S Mount Edgcumbe.

Marshall Ware remembered:
Most of us could swim across the Tamar before we were 16 and we received life-saving training from the Devonport Swimming Club. In those days, boys were allowed to bathe in the nude though I wasn't because my father was a local councillor for the St Budeaux Station Ward so I wasn't allowed to take part in the local activities without a bathing costume. When the women arrived on the scene to bathe, the boys were turned out lock, stock and barrel, often in a state of undress, from the eight bathing cubicles.

A sick note written by Dr Smith on 9th September, 1904. It reads: This is to certify that Phyllis Tozer , Leigh Cottage, Compton, is physically unfit to attend school at any distance over half a mile from her home. AFC Smith.

Marshall Ware remembered:
It was not unusual to see a red flag flying over the house, Meera, in Bull Point Road which was the residence of the area's first resident doctor in 1901. Dr AFC Smith would travel miles in his pony and trap to visit a patient. The red flag signified he was out on his rounds.

This photo shows the building of St Boniface Church. The foundation stone of the church was laid on 4th October, 1911 by the Bishop of Exeter. The Bishop is recorded at the time as saying, 'that although the district was served well by both railway and tramcar, the flow of population had not been quite as rapid as was contemplated when the church and hall were planned.'

The church was consecrated on May 14th, 1913.

The photo shows many cloth capped builders posing for this historical picture. A horse and cart carry some of the men and this is led by two women, one is wearing a straw boater. One of the women appears to be holding a pasty. Oddly, there are two boys on the right of the photo wearing nothing more than their nightshirts.

Marshall Ware remembered:

We had a police station at No 9 Morris Park Terrace (now part of Wolseley Road), almost a stone's throw away from the present office, with Sgt Wallis as our resident officer. His daughter, Mrs Muriel Nevin, lived a few doors away and kept his truncheon, which he never used on the law abiding residents of St Budeaux.

My father, Mr James Ware, was the councillor for Station Ward in the Parish of Devonport, District of Stoke Dameral, until 1914. He introduced the system whereby the County Borough of Devonport's rates could be paid at the police station on Friday from 6-8pm and

the Registrar of births and deaths called earlier on the same day. A system of community policing continued after the Second World War and a police box was placed in St Budeaux Square, right opposite Keith Reid's post office, and a police call box was installed between the Royal Albert and Ferry Inns.
Our local policeman, Emlyn Williams, used to ride a bicycle at regular intervals between the call boxes and report back to HQ.

The police box has now long gone from St Budeaux Square. It would have made an interesting feature if it had been left in place. Unfortunately, police boxes are now few and far between in the UK. Many people will remember the police box that stood on Outland Road for many years until it was removed in the 1970s. The days of police on bicycles returning to police boxes to report in to their headquarters seems a very long time ago now.

Marshall Ware remembered:
Yeoman's Terrace was occupied by several businesses. No 1 was occupied by Mr Truscott, who was a highly respected Baptist. He ran a boot and shoe business. No 3 was occupied by Tom Occleshaw who, in 1901, converted his home into a hairdressing and tobacconist shop. At first, it was lit by oil lamps and later, it boasted that it was the first local shop to be lit by gas lighting. No 4 was a dairy ran by the Menheneott family. Mr Blackmore of Little Ash Farm, sold cream and butter. Also, in Yeoman's Terrace, Mr Eastlake ran a general shop.

A view of St Budeaux Square in the 1950s.

Marshall Ware remembered:
The locals were sorry when the name Occleshaw disappeared from
the scene. Other shops were opened by Mr Truscott, a respected
Baptist, who started a boot makers business and the Menheneotts
opened a dairy. Mr Blackmore sold cream and butter from 1 Yeoman
Terrace and Mr Eastlake had a general shop. A butcher from Ford,
Mr Robertshaw, sold meat from his van on Tuesdays and Saturdays.

Marshall Ware remembered:
The Co-op opened on 1st December, 1895, with Mr W Shepherd as manager followed in 1901 by Mr A D Hammett. He had two assistants and one apprentice who were paid twelve shillings for a sixty hour week.

HMS Acorn in front of the Royal Albert Bridge in 1920. HMS Acorn was a Royal Naval Destroyer and it is shown here waiting to be scrapped. The ship was originally built by John Brown and Company of Clydebank and was launched on 1st July, 1910. It was sold for braking up on May 9th, 1921.

Maurice Dart as a boy at Tamar Terrace.

Railway and history enthusiasts will recognise the name of Maurice Dart who has written many books. Maurice's family moved to St Budeaux in the 1930s and lived at Tamar Terrace.

Maurice Dart remembered:
We moved from Stoke to 16 Tamar Terrace (which later became 52 Normandy Way), during the Spring of 1934, when I was two and a quarter years of age. From Victoria Road, there were only houses on the right side of Vicarage Road, the houses on the left side were built during the following few years. After crossing a rough stony lane at Daymond Road, the two large houses on the right were Waverley Villas followed by the seventeen houses of Tamar Terrace with a small chapel between them. At the bottom end was our 'Back Lane' which then curved to the left and across there was a group of smaller houses on the right which formed Tamar Place. There was one ramshackle building part way along on the left. We had fields at the front and rough ground covered by thickets with fields below and to the lower side at the back. Both were magical places for children to play in. The Mitchells with their daughter Connie and son Peter lived at 1 Waverley Villas. Two sisters each called Miss Moore lived at 17 Tamar Terrace and at 14 lived the Harveys with their sons Cyril and Douglas. Mr.Harvey ran a taxi business and owned two

Austin cars. One from about 1934 had a doubly curved top to it's radiator and was registered BMC 21. This was Mr.Harvey's personal registration and bore the initials of the British Motoring Club. The other which he described as a 'Straight Eight' dated from around 1938 and carried the registration JY 8964. He owned some garages at the bottom of the Back Lane and if the engine of one of the cars required some attention he would take both out but keep the newer car in service. At times, Cyril also did some taxi work. At number 12 lived the Palmers with their daughter Diana and son Carl. At the top end of Tamar Place lived the Rogers with their daughters Betty and Mary. Two doors below them lived the Mays with sons Alan, Bernard and Cyril. These constituted my friends and we all attended Higher St Budeaux Foundation School. Teachers were Miss Ingram (later Mrs Horsham), Miss Williams (later Mrs Cook), Miss Packer, Miss Luckcraft, Mr Cook and two others. The headmaster was Ewart Pryor who was followed by Mr Davey. As well as the playground at the front there was a large playing field at the back of the school. On certain religious days we were taken across the playing field to attend a service in the Parish Church perched at the top of the hill. The boundary ran along the centre of Vicarage Road and when new houses were built on the lower side of the road children living in them had to go down the hill to attend Victoria Road School. Towards the top, east end of Vicarage Road lived the Measons with son Bobby and daughters Betty and Joan. A couple of doors below them were the Hoopers with three sons, the older of whom was Jimmy. They also attended the school 'up the hill'. We walked to school and back twice a day and only caught a bus up in the morning when it was really heavy rain. It was great fun if we found a steam roller on the way home in the afternoon as we walked behind it all of the way up to Mount Tamar and then down the hill. For a couple of Summers before the war, in the afternoon, an ice cream salesman on a tricycle came along our road ringing his bell to attract custom. Before I started attending school, on most days, I was taken up to the 'Rec' (Mount Tamar Recreation Ground) to play on the swings. The Open Air School for delicate children adjoined one side of that. Where Vicarage Road joined Victoria Road there were two shops up a slope on the left. The first was Tappers who sold sweets, newspapers and general goods and next door was Lameys Chemist shop. Opposite on the corner at the junction with Chard Road was a large house called 'SIMLA' which was the surgery and accommodation for our local family GP, Dr Kent, who at first rode a motor bike but then obtained one of the few cars in the area. Going upwards past Mount Tamar, on the left, spaced out were several shops including the St Budeaux Dairy, Higher St Budeaux Post Office and a couple of shops that sold sweets, stationery, books and other goods. When war broke out we were delighted to be able to buy books on aircraft recognition in there. One of them also sold 'Mystery Bags' for about two pence. These would contain sweets such as liquorice, toffees and gums and small toys such as wooden whistles and a cigarette card and were great fun. Going down the hill from the 'corner' as we called the junction with Victoria Road, the first shop on the left on the corner of Lynher Street was Rundles radio shop, which later became Corams Dairy. Peard's newsagent and stationers, who also sold sweets, was on the bottom corner of Evelyn Street. The Masonic Hall was on the top corner of Kathleaven Street and Glen's Fruit and Vegetable shop was between there and Florence Street. Cummings Butchers was on the bottom corner of Florence Street. There was another butchers shop called Kendalls further down the hill. After the war, a group of shops were built on the right going down the hill below Ivanhoe Road the first of which was Goodbodys Bakers. John Bulls Stores and Tierneys Ladies Hairdressers were shops lower down. Below Victoria Road School, on the left, was the library followed by Northcotts Bakery next to which, was the largest shop in the area, the Co-op store. Along Pemros Road, on the left, was Jaspers Newsagents whose daughter was called Brenda. I used to go on errands to all of these for my parents. Friday evening, after my father came home from work, Mum, Dad and I went down to the Co-op to buy groceries for the following week. Sometimes I would take our dog with me and he would patiently wait outside the shop whilst Mr.Cummings found him some bones. Almost every day, before I started going to school, my grandmother, who lived with us, would take me down the hill to St Budeaux GWR station where we would sit down and 'watch trains'. I was taught to memorise the names of three engines we had seen. One day I asked her why we did not go to the Southern Railway station and she replied that they did not have many trains passing and that all of their engines were 'old'. We would also 'watch trains' from our front bedroom window and on one memorable Saturday afternoon I saw a GWR Diesel railcar make one of the type's rare ventures into Cornwall.

We used to go out for walks in the evenings and at weekends. Sometimes these would be to Saltash Passage, at times with a pop over to Saltash on the ferry to buy a bag of prawns.

Maurice Dart by the steps at Saltash Passage

I remember 'The Steps' being built to form a short cut down to the ferry. Also, at Saltash Passage, there was a kiosk which sold sweets and I would go paddling after going down the steps, which still exist, and we would throw sticks into the river for our dog to retrieve. After picking a stick out of the water, he would swim out around the first pier of the Royal Albert Bridge before returning with it. Other walks were to Kings Tamerton and to Weston Mill which was a most interesting place with a water wheel by the mill. As we grew older our little group of boys became more adventurous and we would go up Daymond Road and down the other side to reach what my mother called 'The Piggery'. On several occasions we climbed the gate and went in for a look around and twice we climbed up across the field to reach a path that led farther out to the edge of the high ground overlooking Ernesettle Depot. Here we found two entrances to a tunnel which we explored. One end could only be accessed by lying down and crawling along. Inside were various rooms off the main tunnel and near one of the entrances was a bricked up entrance to a side tunnel which someone said led down to the depot. I wonder if it can still be found? We used to walk towards Kings Tamerton to watch houses being built at Roman Road with excavators and draglines being used and also to watch the developments down towards Fletemoor Road. We also watched the construction of houses on the other side of Vicarage Road, Ivanhoe Road, Waverley Road and Peters Park Lane and kept going down the hill to see the State Cinema being built. At the start of the war, we watched static water tanks and a gas cleansing station being built. Before the war, a fair used to be held opposite where the State was built and we used to spend several evenings there. Dad knew one of the traction engine drivers and I used to go up on the engine and watch the pistons working. When Ivanhoe Road was being built with its houses, Westlake builders erected some sheds halfway down the field on the right and also a lime pit. We used to go down there and play around but were warned to be careful not to fall in the lime pit!

An advert for Dingle and Co, newsagents in the Square in 1928. Interestingly, Mr Dingle later owned the house that I now live in. I've even found some of his discarded items under my floorboards including old Oxo tins, bottles and many newspapers!

This advert for the Tralawny Hotel, the name mis-spelt, appeared in the 1928 programme for the St Budeaux Carnival. The banner announces, 'As popular as ever!' and 'All drinks of the best quality!'

Another advert advertising Dingle and Co's newsagent in the Square. Unusually, they were also a lending library and their advert states, 'Large selection of newest designs in hair slides' which would have been very popular in 1928.

Ray Rylatt remembered:
I was brought up at 18 Scott Avenue, Barn Barton estate, attending Victoria Rd school from about 1937 until leaving in 1946 for Liverpool due to my Dad being stationed at HMS Vivid, Drake and Impregnable. We must have been one of the first families to reside in Scot Avenue in about 1934.
Looking back at my life, St Budeaux and the farmers fields opposite Barn Road to Scott Avenue (sigh, now a housing estate) that we played in. It was the most enjoyable time of my life.

Two

The People

The picture above appeared in the Western Weekly Mercury of the 9th
August 1919 and carried the headline, **'The St Budeaux Carnival'**.
The caption underneath read:

**The Peace Carnival held at Lower St Budeaux on Monday was a
splendid success and gave great enjoyment to thousands. Our
photograph is that of some of those who took part in the day's
proceedings and were attired in fancy dress.**

Also on the front page was a story,carrying the headline, **'St Budeaux
Sports'**. It read:

**In the field attached to the Naval Camp at St Budeaux, the lower St
Budeaux Peace Sports, which were interrupted on Monday by the
bad weather, were continued on Wednesday evening.
The success which attended the celebrations on Bank Holiday
Monday, marked the proceedings again yesterday, and taking into
consideration the spontaneity of the whole affair, great credit is due
to the organisers. Everything had been greatly facilitated by the
kindly co-operation of Commander Armitage and the officers and
ratings of the Naval Camp. P O Stout, as chairman of the Sports
Committee, put in a great deal of hard work.
At the close, Commander Armitage distributed the prizes and a vote
of thanks was passed by the committee to him and his understudies**

for all they had done for St Budeaux. Comander Armitage, in returning thanks, led cheers for the committee, who had 'done all the work'. After the sports, an al fresco entertainment was given by the 'Dons' Concert Party. Messrs Staddon Hancock (sports secretary), and Hare acted as starters. P O Stout (chairman of the Sports Committee) was clerk of the course.

The article then gives the names of people who won various events. These included the 100 yards, the egg and spoon race, catch-the-cockerel, the sack race, the obstacle race, field racing, the blindfold race, the wheelbarrow race, the potato race, thread-the-needle race, the skipping race, the girl's three-legged race, the veterans' race, the 100 yards ladies over 40 race and the committee race. The article also mentioned that in the tug-of-war for boys, the Weston Mill district beat the Saltash Passage district.

The Baptist's Ladies Boating Club holding a model of their boat, Rowena. The Royal Albert Bridge Inn, in Saltash Passage, is in the background. Some older members of the community might recognise some of the faces in this picture. A solitary house stands on Vicarage Road (later Normandy Hill). This section of the road has long since changed with the inclusion of several newer houses.

Helen Wyler remembered:
This is a postcard photo of my grandfather outside 11 Tamar Terrace and his address is written on the back. The postcard is dated 13th September, 1912 and has a message to his wife to be on the back. They married in 1913.

Allotments were very popular especially during the Second World War when people would grow their own food to boost the war effort. Food was in short supply so any piece of extra land that could be cultivated was used to grow vegetables and, perhaps, keep animals such as the pig shown in this picture.

Helen Wyler remembered:
This photo shows my father on a nearby allotment sat on a small wooden stool from the house.

Helen Wyler remembered:
My father appears in this photo aged about 10 to 12 years old. My
Grandfather had a smallholding on which he had a pig and bees.

This photo shows Brenda Jasper at the window of her home on Normandy Hill. Interestingly, the ferry between Saltash Passage and Saltash can be seen in the background. The Jasper family owned the local newsagents.

A coach outing from St Budeaux to Newquay

Two of St Budeaux's oldest residents included Frank and Anita Milford who held the title of Britain's longest married couple. They met when they were both teenagers at a YMCA dance in St Budeaux in 1926.

Anita said, 'We met at a dance in the hut. It isn't even there any more, it's been demolished, which is very sad. I lived a few miles away in Saltash at the time but Frank was a local lad. A few of us girls went to a dance on that night and that's where I met my fate.'

They married two years later at the Torpoint Registery Office on 26th May, 1928.

After their marriage, they lived in a bungalow in St Budeaux and stayed put during the bombing of the Second World War. Their two children, Marie and Frank, were evacuated to the countryside.

Frank had worked as a butcher in his teenage years but worked along side his father from 17 year old, at Devonport Dockyard, until he retired, aged 60.

Anita was a domestic at Tamar House in Saltash.

Mrs Milford said, 'These days, marriages don't last long. A lot of people get married with the idea that if it doesn't work out there's no worry, but we can't understand that.'

They put the secret of their successful marriage down to, 'a little argument every day.' Frank said, ' We always have a kiss and cuddle at night and never go to bed with any bad feeling'.

In later years, Frank's hobbies included gardening, snooker and darts though he had to give up darts as his eye sight failed. They enjoyed meeting friends at the local social club.

Frank said, 'We don't always see eye to eye and we do have a small argument every day. But that comes and goes. We are always here for each other.'

In 2005, they moved to Warwick House Nursing Home. In 2009, when they were both 101, Frank unfortunately died.

Their story was told in October 2009 on BBC Southwest's 'Inside Out' programme.

It's amazing to think how the world has changed since the couple married in 1928. That was the year the first pound note was introduced, King George V was on the throne and Stanley Baldwin was the Prime Minister. A pint of beer cost just 4d.

They lived through great changes including the Second World War, twice narrowly escaping the bombs. One of the bombs hit the dockyard while Frank was on shift but he escaped any injuries.

Members of the local Methodist church.

Maurice Dart on playing fields near his home.

Marshall Ware remembered:
The old St Budeaux Horse Show was a very popular annual event and received widespread support from local farmers and tradesmen. Entries were received for all classes from places as far apart as Liskeard and Totnes. Judges travelled great distances and were given accommodation at the Trelawny Hotel. General Stone was the chairman from 1910 onwards. Mr R Luscombe of Warleigh, Tamerton was a well known breeder of horses and won many of the prizes.

Marshall Ware remembered:
Mrs Cann delivered milk to the area prior to the First World War. She was assisted by her daughter, Mrs Doidge, She served milk not in bottles but by measuring out quantities from the large churns on her cart.

Three
Schools

Many people will remember fondly Victoria Road School and the Foundation School at Higher St Budeaux. Victoria Road School still exists but the Foundation School was demolished many years ago to make way for access to the Parkway which was built in the 1980s.

Marshall Ware remembered:
This photo shows a class at the St Budeaux Foundation School in 1880. In 1843, it was called the St Budeaux Public School.

The children all look very serious in this photo and the teacher on the far left looks quite stern. Perhaps this is misleading though and their straight faces could be a result of waiting patiently for the photographer to take his picture, a new and more complicated process than it is nowadays.

Walter Harris remembered:
When I was eight, we moved from Fowey in Cornwall to St Budeaux when my father became a signalman at the Royal Albert Bridge Box. I attended Victoria Road School until 1940. We lived in Victoria Road opposite St Boniface Church. Later, I became a teacher and taught at the St Budeaux Foundation School between 1950 and 1958.

Victoria Road School in 1905.

A school play at Victoria Road School in 1957. William Hutchinson is the judge. Other costumes in the photo include a sweep, a policeman and a spiv.

Four
Football

Football played a big part of life in St Budeaux and there were many local football teams. These included the Kinterbury Villa team, the Saltash Stars and Woodland Villa. Most of the small teams seemed to disband in the 1920s while some players left to join other teams.

The 1923 Kinterbury Villa team who were winners of the Junior League Cup.

Marshall Ware remembered:
These were the early days of the successful Woodland Villa team who were great rivals of the neighbouring St Budeaux club from 1918 onwards.

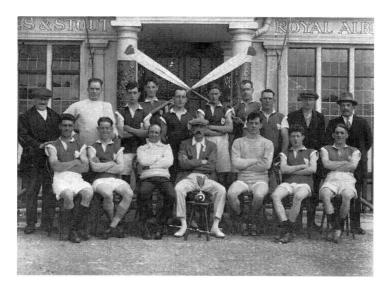

A local football team outside the Royal Albert Bridge Inn. The name of the team has long been forgotten, though perhaps the crossed oars in the background give a clue.

The Lifeboys football team who were undefeated 1956-57.

Mr L Tucker remembered:
I remember the Blue Monkey so well. We played football in the grounds of a lovely little school a few yards down the road. Nearby was the church where my wife and I were married in 1955.

41

Five
Transport

This old photo shows James Ware and his team pictured at Ware's Quay in Saltash Passage.

Marshall Ware remembered:
My father was a carriers' agent, as well as a coal merchant. He had to handle the goods train coming down from the Midlands to deliver shell cases. These were then taken to the Bull Point armaments depot by horse and cart for filling with explosive before being taken out to ships. He and three other carriers had to work almost day and night to handle all those. They shifted 1,309 tons in 1915 and 4,052 tons the following year.
My father was fuel controller for the area during the First World War which was why he resigned from Devonport Town Council in 1914, the year it was merged into Plymouth's.

The railway played a big part in the area with the station at St Budeaux being very busy at one time.
Marshall Ware remembered:
I started using the railway in 1918 to get to school at Plymouth College. That train left St Budeaux Victoria Road and went to Friary and Mutley which is where I got off.

Mr L Tucker remembered:
We had Sunday outings from St Budeaux station to Saltash and
sometimes to Tamerton Foliot. Tamerton Foliot station in Summer
was a picture, no graffiti or rubbish, just beautiful roses, flowers etc
tended by station staff.

A charabanc outing setting off from St Budeaux

Marshall Ware remembered:
I had one of the first cars in Plymouth and I would drive it down into
Saltash Passage. Some of the local children, many who had never
seen a car before, would run along behind chasing it.

Marshall Ware remembered:
In 1890, Mr Edmund Tolley was appointed the first L and S W
Railway station master for St Budeaux. A well loved character, he
will be remembered for occasionally holding up a train in the station
for latecomers.

A one-man operated bus in 1926. Its journey covered the area between Morice Square and Higher St Budeaux.

This photo shows the 12th Plymouth Lifeboys on Church Parade beside St Budeaux Railway Station after the war. The adverts in the background make interesting reading. One is for Goodbody's and says, 'The sign of good bread'. The billboard beside it advertises a box of cakes called, 'Week End'.

L&SWR St Budeaux Victoria Road Station in the 1950's. The station had a friendlier and more welcoming appeal to it in those days.

A steam train passing St Budeaux. The houses in the background are easily recognisable.

A signal changer on the Royal Albert Bridge.

A tram at Saltash Passage. The cobbles and tramlines still remain
beneath the tarmac road that now leads towards Saltash Passage.

Six

The Ferry

The ferry ran for hundreds of years until the building of the Tamar Bridge in 1961.

Philip Syms remembered :
In the days of the Saltash Ferry at the height of the Summer, it wasn't unusual to see the ferry queue all the way back to the Foulston Avenue junction and, on the odd occasion, up to the St. Budeaux bridge, so if you knew how many vehicles the ferry held it was easy to know how many hours they had to wait.

Graham Sullivan remembered:
I spent my first five years living in St. Budeaux, (Kathleven Street 1946-1950) and every summer holiday at Peters Park Lane there afterwards. My time in the summer holidays was spent nearly every day at the Passage and spending my penny to cross to Saltash. My friends and I did have our fare back but, being kids, we had a better use for the return penny! We were never challenged for the return fare, even though we crept onto the ferry so quietly nobody could ever have heard us (usually four to six in number), creeping around the ferry in advance of the ticket collector. To this day, I'll never know how they missed us all! I remember the ticket collector, or rather the ticket collector's uniform. A ticket machine, white coat and white top hat - just like the Plymouth C.C.T. drivers and conductors. The Winter ferry used to be stabled about half way between the bridge and the Passage running jetty. I have seen elsewhere discourse on the ferry colours. They were Battleship Grey over black.

Seven
The Regatta

The Regatta was an annual event greatly looked forward to by the residents of St Budeaux and the surrounding areas. Combined with Little Ash Tea Gardens, it attracted thousands of people to the area.

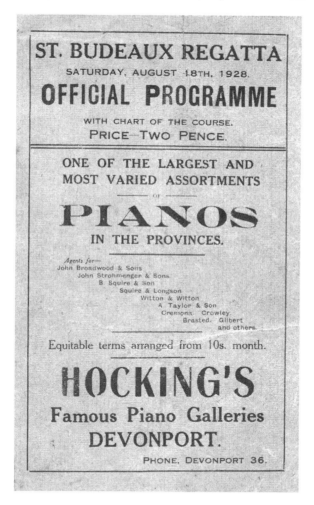

The cover of the official programme for the St Budeaux Regatta which took place on Saturday 18th August 1928.

Two very grainy photos of the 1919 St Budeaux Carnival.
The Western Weekly Mercury reported the event in its edition of Saturday 9th August, 1919. The caption read:

The amusement part of the programme was well provided for. Those shown in this group caused roars of laughter as the procession proceeded through the town.

Shown in this photo are clowns, jesters, a policeman, a brick layer, farmers, a cavalier, a chef etc. Many people have their faces blackened with boot polish, which would probably be frowned upon nowadays. However, another man has whitened his face.

The Western Weekly Mercury caption for this photo read:

A group of the officials who arranged the excellent carnival which took place in St Budeaux on Monday.

These include many women of the community, the two local bobbies and the bus driver.

You can get a splendid view from

Little Ash Tea Gardens

Of the St. Budeaux Regatta.

—: Refreshments at Moderate Prices :—

IN THE PAVILION.

An advert for Little Ash Tea Gardens featured in the 1928 St Budeaux Regatta programme.

Older local residents remember Little Ash Tea Gardens at the top of what was to become Little Ash Gardens. One resident remembers that the gardens had a fairground galloper, a beautiful carousel complete with horses. However, while most carousels were usually colourfully decorated, the one at Little Ash Tea Gardens was painted completely grey.

Little Ash Tea Gardens.

Marshall Ware remembered the old blacksmith's at Kings Tamerton.

Marshall Ware remembered:
I remember the old cob-built cottage and the adjoining building
decorated with pieces of pottery, china and glass. Mr Charlie
Deacon's old blacksmith shop at Kings Tamerton was built on the
old Saltash Road, which was the main road from Plymouth to the
Saltash Ferry. Mr Deacon lived with his family in the adjoining
Traveller's Rest, an old time hostelry.
He was an expert shoeing smith and had a wonderful way with
horses. It came as a shock to the neighbourhood when the
blacksmith went out shooting rabbits late one evening, fell in a well
and was killed.
Charlie Deacon's sons, George and Alf, carried on the business until
the Plymouth Corporation took over the property and adjoining land
for new housing estates.

Charlie Deacon's early demise was later raised in another item that
appeared in the local paper. It read:

The story about Charlie Deacon, one-time blacksmith at King's
Tamerton, who was reputed to have met his death through falling
down a well, while out rabbiting, is an ill-founded legend.
I have this from one of his granddaughters , Mrs Sylvia Griffin, of

Bittaford.

She writes : 'I feel I must put the record straight. Our grandfather did not meet an untimely end. He did, in fact, live to the grand age of 84 and died peacefully in his sleep at his home in Roman Way, St Budeaux, where he moved when the blacksmith's shop was taken over by Plymouth Corporation.'

Mrs Griffin is the youngest of Mr Deacon's five granddaughters. She tells me that while he did do a lot of rabbiting, the well incident is just a myth.

'I have no idea how this story got about.' she said. Mr Deacon used to sell the rabbits for the pot for 3d each and got extra for the skins.

Mr L Tucker remembered:

I remember the coal merchant and his horse and there were other deliveries and collections which were horse drawn. There was the man who used to sharpen knives and scissors.

William Hutchinson with his parents at Bull Point in 1953. The Royal Albert Bridge can be seen in the background on the left of the picture.

An early photo of Tamar Terrace later renamed Normandy Way after the American servicemen who passed this way during the Second World War.

Helen Wyler remembered:
This photo is of the front garden of 11 Tamar Terrace. The boy is my brother and it was taken about 1952. He remembers riding a bike in the wasteland opposite the house.

Eight

The Second World War

Ray Rylatt and his brother, Douglas, wearing tin hats and carrying their gas masks. Behind them is the entrance to the air raid shelter in their garden.

Ray Rylatt remembered:
Behind my brother, Douglas, is the shelter entrance facing towards the clothes line pole. Stretching back to his right, covered in turf, was where soon after Mother had the shelter dug up and placed closer to the house as it was faster to get into it rather than run down the path!

Ray Rylatt remembered:
At the top of Barn Road, the council houses finished on the right and a farmer's field started and then there was a small copse of trees which we called the 'quarry'. Many a day, we played in that 'forest' with our imaginations going wild. Opposite the copse were the fields belonging to the farmer. On one day, we went to play there and the left side had been flattened and it had become a bus parking lot for the Dockyardies from Bull Point. Near the same place, a road had

been built to HMS Impregnable to accommodate many new Nissan huts for the incoming sailors from all over the 'Empire' . I do remember a very young sailor, with 'Fiji' written on his shoulder wanting to play football with us and he would often meet us in the field until, one day, he disappeared. I guess he left. The road leading down to the 'Fort' and 'Mud Cap' from the quarry had a machine that belched out black smoke when air raids occurred. Darn policemen never let us past so we always cut through the quarry when strolling to Mud Cap to play in the Tamar bay. We used to take the steep steps leading down to the Mud Cap from the road leading to Saltash Passage just before the bend to the right.

Ray Rylatt remembered:
I recall that Bull Point had put all their ammo in barges in the middle of the Tamar for safer storage. A stray bomb hit one and the air raid shelter we were in shook with the force of the explosion. We assumed a bomb had landed on our house or close by. Next morning, Scott Avenue, and the field nearby, were littered with pieces of shrapnel. In the field, we came across a 5-8 ft piece of twisted barge siding. The soldiers and airmen from the ack-ack guns and balloon camp came down to clear up.

The ammunition barge explosion is well remembered and affected much of Saltash Passage and the surrounding area. Many of the ceilings in the nearby houses came down. One resident living at Normandy Hill recalled hearing the explosion at night and not thinking anymore of it and upon waking in the morning found part of a barge in his front garden. Marshall Ware recalled that there were bodies up in the trees near to The Kloof from the explosion which he said, 'upset him awfully'.

Maurice Dart remembered:
I was a child living at 16 Tamar Terrace, Higher St Budeaux, Plymouth, when war was declared. My grandmother lived with my parents and myself in a terraced house overlooking the River Tamar and the Admiralty Shore base, which I think we called HMS Impregnable.
We heard on the radio about the invasion of Poland and the German atrocities, so received the news of war with a mixture of apprehension and awe. What will the Germans do to us if they come, we wondered. Preparations for defence commenced.
When war broke out we had to demolish the old wooden shed in the back garden, dig a large hole and erect an Anderson Shelter. I helped my father pull down a wooden shed in the garden, releasing many large spiders in the process, after which we dug a pit in the garden and put up an Anderson Air Raid shelter. I likened this to a huge Meccano set. We covered the shelter with several layers of earth and Dad built a porch on to the front of the shelter fitted with a side door. This was to lessen the effects of blast from bombs. He also installed electric lighting and being a Joiner by trade, he built in bunk beds for us. Sticky tape was placed diagonally across all of our windows and blackouts, made from wood or from thick black curtains, were fitted to each window. Buckets filled with sand and water were placed outside the back of the house and in the roof space and we obtained a stirrup pump.
Gas masks were issued to everyone and at school gas mask drill was carried out twice a day. Great emphasis was placed on this, as there was anticipation of gas attacks from the air. A gas mask procession proceeded through Plymouth, which many people watched. Men wearing gas masks wheeled handcarts and tied on to each of them was a Winchester quart glass bottle containing a liquid, some of which was coloured, each labelled with the name of a poison gas.

Dad obtained some extra pieces of corrugated iron and built a sideways porch on to the front of the shelter to keep out the effects of 'Blast'. We were told that if we were out when the air raid warning sounded, we were to go into the nearest house and ask to use their shelter. This happened once when I was on the way home from school and I went to a house in Clifford Terrace and sheltered though no plane was heard. When the second raid took place, I was at home and Mum, Gran and I went to the shelter around 4.30pm. Soon, we heard a plane and one bomb dropped nearby. After 'All Clear' had sounded we went back into the house and as we had been drilled, carried out an inspection of each room. We reached the last room which was my parent's front bedroom and found large chunks of the ceiling lying on the bed and on the floor and a big dust cloud floating around. The bomb had dropped two fields behind us and one piece of shrapnel had lodged in our roof and had brought the ceiling down. During the Blitz raids, an incendiary bomb fell on ours and our neighbours roofs but they were extinguished by the local male residents, including my father, using stirrup pumps and sand. Each morning we would walk around viewing damage in the neighbourhood. We boys also collected 'souvenirs' which included pieces of shrapnel, incendiary bomb tails, pieces of flares, machine gun bullet clips, Pom-Pom rounds and all manner of other items, some of which were very heavy, jagged and sharp! After one night of heavy bombing, we walked up to Verna Road to look at a house where the side had been blown off exposing the bath sitting in position. Sometimes roads would be roped off and a 'Danger Unexploded Bomb' notice would be displayed. One night Dad came home from 'Fire Watching' on the roof of the Victualling Yard and told us that there was a bus upside down on the roof of Milehouse Depot and that an engine had been blown on to the platform at Keyham. We walked down to the Square to view the damage to the railway houses and the stations. There was a triangle of grass as one went down Stirling Road on the lower side of which was a small shop which always had a very good selection of fireworks in the week leading up to 5th November. About a year after war broke out an Anti-Aircraft Gun Battery was erected on the triangle of grass. During the Blitzes we would occasionally say 'Oh, that was our gun going off'. When both of the schools were bombed in April 1941, I, along with many other pupils, was evacuated to Bude. By the time I returned from evacuation for a few months in 1943, the Americans had established a large camp at Vicarage Road just before the hill down to Saltash Passage. We would go there by the gate and wait and the American troops would give us sweets, chocolates and other items such as cocoa, butter and eggs. My mother reprimanded me for going there but she was pleased to receive the few 'extras'. I was home on school holidays to see many of the troops marching past on their way to Saltash Passage to embark for the D-Day Landings.

The Vicarage Road Camp.

Pat Twyford remembered:
August 27,1940. Raiders dropped a trail of bombs across the fields at Higher St Budeaux, missing in a most amazing way the new reservoir, the ancient parish church in which Sir Francis Drake was married, and many houses. Budshead Farm, down in the valley, had a remarkable escape.

Residents in Pemros Road recall two Messerschmitts flying along the Tamar and firing their guns along the road leaving large furrows in the ground.

Marshall Ware remembered:
There were 100 homes in the Saltash Passage postal area. It started from the post box behind the bus stop at 790 Wolseley Road to the Royal Albert Bridge Inn, in fact, all the houses south of the Southern Railway Line.

The area was considered very vulnerable, wedged between Ernesettle Depot, the Royal Albert Bridge and Bull Point. In particular, Little Ash Gardens and the twelve bungalows and two houses squeezed in the quarry were very vulnerable and a fragmentation bomb could have caused disaster. An enlarged map with all the names of the residents in Little Ash Gardens was held at the St Budeaux First Aid Post.

Some of the precautions taken in Saltash Passage included; the protection of the stained glass windows of St Peters Mission Church with sand bags, two pill boxes built on the quay to protect the Royal Albert Bridge, an air raid shelter built in the quarry for those caught out in air raids, provision of static water tanks by auxiliary fire service and a Royal Observer Post in the field of Little Ash Farm.

Pat Twyford remembered:

August 28,1940. During last night, six bombs and a few incendiaries were dropped in the country between Higher St Budeaux and Crownhill. Incendiaries which threatened the woodlands were quickly dealt with by the Auxiliary Fire Service. The high explosive bombs did no damage of any serious consequence.

Marshall Ware remembered:

Duffryn Cottage, now 796 Wolseley Road, had its air raid shelter hit by a fragmentation bomb. Nancy, Kate, Elizabeth and Mary were killed. Also, Cross Trees Bungalow, now 802 Wolseley Road, was destroyed by a blast. Mrs Nuttall and her married niece were killed though Mr Eli Nuttall had a lucky escape.

Mr L Tucker remembered:
I was in Barne Road during the war spending many nights in an Anderson shelter. One large bomb landed in the field opposite, no more than 50 yards away, and blew in the windows of the house.

Maurice Dart remembered:
From 1937, I attended Higher St Budeaux Foundation School. It was up the hill, one mile from our home. I went home to dinner and usually walked each way unless it was heavy rain, when I used a bus. Air Raid practices were carried out and we were told to get to a shelter fast when the sirens sounded. I began to learn Aircraft Recognition, at which I became very proficient. Then came a few daylight raids, one of which was as I was walking home for tea. We had been told that if we were out doors when the siren sounded to run into the nearest house to seek shelter, in case an enemy plane attempted to machine gun us. During one of the early raids a lone raider dropped one bomb, attempting to hit the Royal Albert Bridge but the bomb landed above Ernesettle, two fields away from our house and the blast shook our shelter. On emerging from the shelter, after the All Clear had sounded, we gazed around the outside of the house to check if any damage had occurred. Nothing could be seen so went indoors and proceeded to inspect each room,

as we had been instructed to do. Downstairs was all right so we went upstairs and on entering the front bedroom we found the ornamental ceiling had come down. Large pieces were on the bed, with clouds of dust in the air and masonry all over the place. Our war had arrived. We gazed at it speechless and trembling, and Mum cried a little. Dad arrived home from the Dockyard and scaled the roof. He came back down with a large piece of shrapnel from the high explosive bomb that had caused the damage. We cleared up the mess with assistance and the bedroom was moved to the downstairs front room. The ceiling was repaired within a week, but without the ornamentation. Dad turned the cupboard under the stairs into a makeshift shelter for use at night in bad or cold weather. As the raids intensified, this was deemed unsafe and we went up the garden to the Anderson. I had a zip-up siren suit that I had to don very quickly. We started collecting souvenirs. These were pieces of shrapnel, incendiary bomb tails, bits of shells, pieces of flares, machine gun bullet clips, etc. Each boy had a "box of bits" some of which were quite heavy and razor sharp.

One afternoon whilst looking out of our downstairs front room window I heard a plane and machine gun fire. I watched in awe as each of the three barrage balloons over Impregnable caught fire and fell earthwards. As the third was igniting the Air Raid warning sounded. No bombs were dropped and the raider vanished.

From September 1940, I transferred to Victoria Road School down the hill. Dad had become an Air Raid Warden and carried out Fire Watching on the roof of the Victualling Yard at Stonehouse as well as in our locality, several nights a week.

As the raids intensified two additional signals were given. These were 'Imminent Danger', which was short sharp fast beeps and 'Danger Passed', which was long spaced out beeps. On several, occasions, Imminent Danger sounded concurrent with the sirens. Very noticeable was the stillness after the sirens had sounded, only broken by dogs howling, until the planes arrived. Also, there was a pronounced silence for a while after the All Clear sounded.

Sometimes during a raid, one would hear a fighter engaging raiders with machine guns chattering. We had been told that new Boulton Paul Defiant two seat night fighters were at Harrowbeer to defend the city. Then, in March 1941, came the Blitzes, first Plymouth for several nights and a week or so later, Devonport and St Budeaux. These were frightening times, although our family escaped injury. We had a couple of Incendiaries in our roof, both of which were extinguished successfully. Imminent Danger would be sounding as the sirens were wailing and we raced to the shelter in night clothes, with planes above and guns firing at them. The noise consisted of planes, gunfire, whistling bombs and land mines exploding, with pauses between different waves of raiders. An Ack-Ack gun had been installed on a piece of open ground a quarter of a mile from our house, near the Royal Albert Bridge, and at times during a raid we would occasionally say, 'That was our gun'. In the daytime, we would venture out shopping to find wholesale destruction, but shops would open again in temporary premises, especially around Devonport. Areas would be roped off with a notice stating 'Danger! Unexploded Bomb'. Emergency kitchens sprung up on street corners in Plymouth, Devonport, and Ford and we went to see a crashed Dornier bomber in the Milehouse area. Gas and electricity were cut off for days and Gran was in her element. She had been an army cook in the early 1900s at Chatham and rubbed her hands together and said, 'Oh, I can get my good old coal stove going and cook on that.' It was her pride and joy and she used it to cook for eight families for three weeks. We were given extra supplies of coal to keep the stove going. Our relatives were bombed out three times, at Stoke and Devonport, and that family of four lived with us for several months. Dad would come home from Fire Watching with stories of damage. He would be tired out and sobbing at the destruction, and tell us, 'All of the dockyard's on fire!'

A great many schools had been bombed including Victoria Road, so the decision was taken to evacuate schoolchildren from the city. We had to report to Higher St Budeaux School and take a letter to our parents. The next day I was packed off with a suitcase, gas mask, and identity label, on a bus to Friary station and we departed by train for an unknown destination, which turned out to be Bude. We were taken to a reception centre, split into groups, and taken by car to various houses to find us billets. I was 'taken in' by a farmer and his wife on the outskirts of the town a short distance from the farm. Here I grew up and developed a North Cornish accent. We had a combined school formed from the two St Budeaux schools and our schoolroom was on the other side of the town at Flexbury, so I walked a mile four times a day, as I had done at St Budeaux. We seemed to spend large amounts of time going to the beach instead of having lessons and I told Dad. He came up and transferred me to Bude Junior School from where I later took my scholarship exam which I passed.

At Bude, we played soldiers, had bows and arrows, toy guns and model aeroplanes, and we all wanted to 'beat the Germans'. Our parents visited us periodically. Cleeve Aerodrome was nearby and we once saw a flight of Beaufighters practicing low-level flying. On another occasion, we saw a flight of Dornier 17 'Flying Pencils' in the distance but no siren sounded. For a couple of days a Messerschmitt 109 fighter, that had been shot down, was displayed on the Green at Bude. Many American troops were stationed in the area around Bude. Their large lorries were a familiar sight. I returned to Plymouth at Easter 1943 and rejoined Higher St Budeaux Foundation School. I remember large water pipes at Mutley Plain, Crownhill, St Budeaux Square and various other places, laid in the gutters on each side of the road. We had to step up and over these to board buses. We experienced more air raids. Mum had joined the WVS and worked two days a week in the Food Office, which was near Blindman's Wood.

In September 1943, I joined Sutton High School and was evacuated to St Austell until the end of the war. I spent a few months in a billet at Tregonissey before moving into a school hostel in 'Trelawny'. This was a large house at the end of Tremena Road that accommodated thirty eight boys with one Housemaster and his wife. Evacuated and living in a school hostel resembled attending a boarding school and really shaped us up. I became a St John's Ambulance Cadet and still specialised in Aircraft Recognition. One feature of our school life at St Austell was that our schoolrooms were scattered between various buildings. They were at Trevarthian, the Old Town Hall, Mengu, St Johns, and Church Rooms, in the town, whilst we went to West Hill School for metalwork, Bridge Chapel for woodwork and to the County School for chemistry and physics. Because of this, there were constant streams of Suttonians passing through Fore Street en route between these. We returned to Plymouth for holidays sometimes and when the war was over, although not until mid-August 1945, several weeks after the school term had ended.

In 1944, Dad obtained a Cocker Spaniel called Scamp who would accompany Gran in the Anderson shelter. Since the onset of the Blitzes, Gran slept in the shelter each night until the war ended. Early in 1944, Dad went to Gibraltar to work in the Dockyard. He sailed from Greenock and the voyage took about seven weeks as the boat took a devious route to avoid U-Boats.

So, in August 1945, living at St Budeaux were Gran, Mum, and 'Her two young Scamps', as she put it. One of them, of course, was me! I had been aged seven and a half when war broke out and it seems a very long time ago now!

Pat Twyford remembered:
October 23,1940. A single German raider dropped four highly explosive bombs between Moor Lane and St Budeaux. There were no casualties and only slight damage.

This photo taken at the Vicarage Road Camp shows some of the survivors from the Slapton Sands exercise in April 1944. Pictured are Alexander Brown, Tom Clark, Fred Beattie, Ed Panter, James Murdock, Gene Eckstam, Bernard Carey, Doug Harlander and Scoffy Gill. They were later sent to Exeter for new uniforms and then sent to different detachments in readiness for D Day.

Marshall Ware remembered:
Early in 1942, a construction firm wanted to build an oil tank on Little Ash Farm in Saltash Passage. As my roots went back to 1906, they thought that I would be able to recommend a site. It was decided to approach the selected site through Little Ash Gardens and move the pipe and large metal sections by a large crane and lay pipes to St Budeaux Wharf where oil barges piped the oil to the tank. The oil was then fed to the tank landing craft, attached to the five groynes, by gravity feed.

A very rare photo of the US troops leaving Saltash Passage.

Ray McSweeney remembered:
This photo shows Major Glenn Miller meeting Sam Donohue. This photo wasn't taken in Plymouth although these two did meet up in the city. Sam led the Artie Shaw Naval Band based at the Vicarage Road USN Camp. Sam and several of the band members were in films and backed Frank Sinatra post war. The dance hall was next door to the Cornwall's Gate Inn.

CERTIFICATE OF RESIDENCE

Serial No. *4708*

FOR PERSONS WHOSE IDENTITY CARDS BEAR AN ADDRESS WITHIN THE AREA.

1. M*rs Dorothy HANCOCK* (name)

of *7, Oreomini Bungalow* *Saltash Passage.* (address)

whose National Registration Identity Card No. is

W E UT/11/91 3.

is hereby certified to be a resident within the area specified in the Schedule to Direction No. 3 under Defence Regulation 18A by the General Officer Commanding-in-Chief, Southern Command.

VALIDITY :—UNTIL FURTHER NOTICE provided the place of residence remains unchanged. This certificate MUST be surrendered in the event of a change of address.

2. This certificate must be carried out of doors at all times and shown on demand together with the holder's Identity Card to any Constable or member of His Majesty's or Allied Forces on duty.

Signature of holder *Dorothy Hancock*

For the Chief Constable of

Date *19th april 1944*

S.C.P. 104. 1,200 pads of 8(?) 1SIP(?)542 9 8-44

Marshall Ware remembered:
We all had identity cards but Saltash Passage residents were issued with yellow Certificate of Residence Cards. It bore the holder's National Registration Identity Card number and stated that the holder was hereby certified to be a resident within the specified area and that it must be carried out of doors at all times and shown to any Constable or member of His Majesty's or Allied Forces on duty. It bore the signature of the holder and was signed by the Chief Constable of Plymouth and the distribution was completed by 19th April 1944.
One resident, wearing tennis gear, forgot to carry his card and was taken in a jeep for interrogation to the US Naval Advanced Amphibious Base at Vicarage Receiving Barracks at St Budeaux.

A very rare photo of the US troops leaving from Saltash Passage. The Royal Albert Bridge Inn is in the background and the white building, that is now a cafe, can also be seen.

The smiling faces of the US troops leaving from Saltash Passage for D-Day in 1944. I hope they made it back. They seem so happy and you can imagine why they were so popular with the local population especially the children of the area who would pester them for sweets and chewing gum. The operation was, of course, so secretive, that few photos exist of the troops during their time spent at Saltash Passage and I was very lucky to have been sent these few by Ray Mc Sweeney.

American troops leaving from Saltash Passage in 1944. Photos of the US Army in Saltash Passage are extremely rare and I would be surprised if any others exist.

A later photo showing the US Base at Vicarage Road. The tin huts are clearly visible as is the white flag pole in the foreground.

Maurice Dart remembered:
I remember the American's camp at Vicarage Road. When I was a boy, we would go down to the gate sometimes and they would give us chocolates and sweets and items to take home, such as tins of cocoa, biscuits and butter. My mother used to tell me off for scrounging but she was pleased to receive it all!

Ray Rylatt remembered:
At the beginning of the Second World War, they installed a RAF Balloon and Army AA battery on top of the hill. Many a time we would cross the fields to talk and, at times, play soccer with the soldiers. Your website has rekindle many a memory. especially of the Terrace House in Higher St Budeaux. It was the first house my brother and I went to see on a Sunday afternoon instead of attending St Boniface. I also remembered the bomb, it was said at the time that it was a land mine, that landed between the Southern Railway bridge and the police kiosk (that was in the middle of the Square) cutting off the road.

An aerial shot of the Vicarage Road Camp in 1945. Although this photo
was taken after the war, the Nissan huts of the camp can still be seen on
the right of the picture. Also the American built hards used to leave for
D- Day are still in place. The camp was decommissioned on 25th
August,1945.

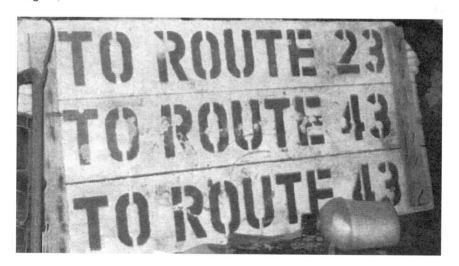

Marshall Ware remembered:
The Royal Observer Corps had an observation post on Little Ash Farm which was occupied by the Americans. They also occupied 900 Wolseley Road, Saltash Passage, because it stood right behind the five groynes. The Americans moved the Stoneman family to number 9 Little Ash Gardens and they built a marquee on their large garden. For many years after the Americans left, I had the large heavy timber Route March Boards with No 23 for the Vicarage Route and No 43 for the Saltash Passage Route. They are now kept at the Royal Albert Bridge Inn.

Ray Rylatt remembered:
At the bottom of Barn Road estate, opposite the fish and chip shop, the butchers and confectionary stores, was a high brick wall and behind it was the orchard. They had built into the wall and below the orchard was a concrete air raid shelter. A small bomb was dropped into the orchard which just missed the shelter. Another shelter was built into the retaining wall on the left hand side just before the Southern Railway bridge that crossed the main road to Devonport and Plymouth, after you leave St Budeaux, before the entry to 'Shaky Bridge' over the Camels Head part we called, 'Stinky Bay'. I believe it is now filled in and is part of HMS Drake.
In the middle of St Budeaux Square was the local policeman's mini police station! It always seemed to be the same policeman, very grey. He kept the traffic at bay when we crossed the street near Dewhursts butchers and the Co-operative cake shops. On our way to Victoria school, I also remember the Southern Railway Station Shop where two ladies served sweets etc.
How well I remember Saltash Passage, we played there and caught shrimps by the car ferry. We sat on a wall to the left of the ferry entry behind the house, I think it was a walk way to the rear of the houses and to the right was the standby ferry and later in the war lots of USA landing craft with sailors who gave us packages of waxed boxes of dried eggs and potatoes!
We would cross the ferry to Saltash to go swimming in a very cold almost square, swimming pool below the railway bridge that was operated by an old man. He let the water in when the tide was high. The small shop to the left, after getting off the ferry, sold cockles which were very tasty. Once, in Spring, we went cycling on the road leaving Saltash and went right to go primrose and bluebell picking for our mothers.

Philip Syms remembered:

There used to be an air raid shelter in front of the houses past Fletemoor Road. At the age of about twelve I used to play in them with my mates. Inside was just a concrete seat with wooden slats running the full length of the shelter. It was built at the beginning of the war, mainly for service personnel and dockyard workers as most of them would walk to the barracks and dockyard and, of course, anyone who should be passing at the time of an air raid.

The air raid shelter is still there today, though sealed up. On close inspection you can see where the entrances have been bricked up and a ventilation hole has been left.

Its location is past Fletemoor Road. There are then a row of six or eight semi-detached council houses fronted by a rising pathway with a handrail. After that, continuing up this path is a row of fourteen semi-detached private houses. These private houses were the original Wolseley Road, numbers 1 to 14 (I lived in No. 3). Late in the 1950's, they were renumbered and Wolseley Road suddenly stretched from Milehouse to Saltash Passage (number 3 suddenly became 578).

Directly in front of these private houses is an embankment with a steep slope to the main road. What appears to be a retaining wall at road level is actually the old air raid shelter.

The 29th, all with smiling faces, leaving for D-Day in 1944. Unfortunately, many would later be killed.

Nine
After the War

Philip Syms remembered:

My earliest recollections were in 1945. My father, Frederick, was away at war. I was five years old and about to start school at Camels Head Primary School. I distinctly remember it as my mother Mary took me by the hand and walked me there and I cried all the way. On arrival at the school, I was met by my first teacher, Mrs Kent, a short, grey haired lady who desperately tried to settle me and a few others down. Matters were to be made worse when the moment arrived when my mother had to leave. At the time, I thought I was being abandoned.

After a few weeks, I began to make my own way to and from school. I always looked forward to the walk home because I would stop at the sharp bend in the road where Carlton Terrace joined Bridwell Road as there was a bridge over the Southern Railway where I used to wait for a train that came along at that time.

Back then in 1945, the engines were steam and as the engine passed beneath the bridge smoke would come billowing out of its funnel and, for a few moments, I was lost in all the smoke, I used to think it smelled wonderful. At the bottom of Carlton Terrace, where it joined the main road to Camels Head, was a tall Nissan type shed which was a garage where you could get petrol . Prior to it being a garage this shed used to house two trams.

My walk would then continue through the allotments which would eventually bring you to Cardinal Avenue where there were a couple of houses that were damaged during the war by incendiary bombs, then down the steep hill into Borringdon Avenue where I would finally arrive at the rear entrance of 3 Wolseley Road where I lived.

One day, whilst at school, I remember American soldiers arriving and going around all the classrooms handing out to all the children a bag of sugar and a bag of cocoa powder, a good will gesture to take home to our parents (food rationing wasn't on their agenda). Well, having a sweet tooth, I was in my element. All the way home it was a case of ' wet finger, dip in cocoa, wet finger dip in sugar' and repeat this action as long as necessary. By the time I arrived home about a quarter of it had disappeared and the tell tale clue to it's whereabouts was all around my mouth!

In 1946 my father Frederick returned from the war. I don't recall

Fred Syms

being excited, probably because I couldn't remember him as I was so small the last time that he saw me. What I do recall, was a man arriving at our home, a man who I had seen in photographs shown to me by my mother. On his arrival, he gave me a wooden train. All it was were three or four pieces of wood (something like fire chopsticks) , smoothed off and hooked together. The windows, doors and wheels were neatly drawn on in ink and when it was all hooked up it looked amazing. My father was very good at using his imagination and I had a new toy.

Looking back, I should have been over the moon at his arrival but, at that age, one doesn't comprehend. Unbeknown to me at the time, I was one of the lucky ones as there were thousands of youngsters who never knew their fathers as they never returned from the war.

Helen Wyler remembered:

The drive to Plymouth from Bucks seemed endless for me as a young child in the mid 1950s and early 1960s. There were no motorways, but no seat belts either, so I expect the boredom resulted in frequent bouts of mischief from my brother and me in the back seat.

Our destination was 11, Tamar Terrace (or was it 62, Normandy Way by then?) – Grandma and Grandpa Robertson's house. They had married quite late, and I had also arrived quite late to their son John, so they were 70 and 80 respectively when I was born. On the earliest photo I have (taken in their front garden) I was aged about one, and we continued our yearly visits till I was 8, when Grandma died in the former Freedom Fields Hospital in 1963. Grandpa had died in 1957, and I barely remember him.

Their house still features in my dreams. It seemed vast. A stern brolly and hat stand in the hallway, horsehair-stuffed sofa and armchairs, round walnut dining table, lots of pictures, flowery furnishings and rugs. The furniture seemed weighty, solid, self-important and permanent, compared to the more 'fashionable' lightweight furniture of the 1950's and 60's favoured by my parents at the time.

Going to bed was an adventure. The room (facing the front) was very dark compared to my room at home. Much, much later, I realised this was because it still had the war-time blackout blinds behind the curtains. I was never afraid there and I think this was because despite a lack of overt affection on my grandparents' part, the house exuded a feeling of safety and solidity. There was a tiny light, suspended from the ceiling, near my bed, which I had thought was put there especially for me to keep me company when alone at bedtime. I have since been told that it was probably a low wattage light for use during blackouts – if such things existed. It certainly made bedtime more comforting than at home, and I never feared monsters behind the curtains there!

In 1951 (according to archives), my grandparents got planning permission for a loft extension comprising two rooms. This was a fascinating 'extra dimension' for me to explore. I only remember one of the rooms, which was full of unfamiliar objects: piles of circular hat boxes, rolls of material, a dress-making dummy, and large trunks, which I dared not open, and whose secret contents were wrapped in stillness and dust-laden sunbeams. I suspect I was not supposed to go up there, as I remember tiptoeing around, taking care to replace things exactly where they had been!

A steam train travelling toward the Royal Albert Bridge in 1956. In the background can be see the Army camp at Vicarage Road.

Philip Syms in his garden in 1943.

Philip Syms remembered the St Budeaux and District Gardeners Association:
My mother, Mary Syms, was a great organiser and in about 1943, Mary and two friends, Bob Couch and Ted Fry, both teachers, got together and formed a gardening club which became very popular and was soon known as the St Budeaux & District Gardeners Association.
When it first started, Bob Couch stored all the fertilizers and seeds in the front room of his house in Edith Street, St Budeaux, where trading took place every Sunday morning and the gardening meetings were held at Victoria Road School. Membership began to grow very quickly and meetings regularly saw 120 members attending with the annual membership fee being two shillings.
Before long a plot of land in Peters Park Lane, at the junction of Ferrers Road and Colebrook Road was rented and a Nissan hut was erected on a concrete slab which became the association's store. My father, Frederick, became the trading secretary and Mary the Secretary.

Mary Syms

Management meetings were held at my parents home (then 3 Wolseley Road) and annual shows were held at various locations over the years including St Budeaux Baptist Chapel, Higher St Budeaux Foundation School and St Budeaux Methodist Church (opposite the State cinema).

In 1960, the Nissan hut in Peters Park Lane was replaced by a permanent building. This site was very convenient for many gardeners as immediately to the rear of the building was a large piece of land which was sectioned off into something like 50 or 60 allotments.

The association was entered many times for the Devon County quiz and several times St Budeaux won. Trips were also organised to places such as Budleigh Salterton to see famous gardens.

On the 1st of November 1963 , Mary and Frederick were both granted life honorary membership by the St Budeaux and District Gardeners Association in appreciation for the long, loyal and valuable service they had given over the years. Both received plaques signed by the President at the time, A E Mardon.

Graham Sullivan remembered:

Most visits we'd break the shale off on the little bank underneath the bridge on the Passage side to 'skim' across the river. Today I'm not sure if we'd be classed as vandals or recyclers! I took my son there some years ago and we recycled some more!

The Baptist's Ladies Boating Club with their boat, 'Rowena', at Saltash Passage on 30th June, 1947. The 'hards' laid down by the American servicemen in 1944 can be seen in the foreground. The building, by the ferry slip way in the background, shows damage to the roof from enemy bombing during the war. The front has now changed a bit and the building on the right of the picture has now gone and has been replaced by the yacht club. The area will be instantly recognisable to most residents of St Budeaux and the houses in the background have changed little over the years.

Philip Syms remembered shops and premises during the 1940's and 1950's :

At the junction of Fleetmoor Road and St Budeaux was the Baptist Chapel which was built in a hollow and whenever it rained very heavily water would run down from Fleetmoor Road and all the adjoining streets and the same would happen with water from Borringdon Avenue, Barn Barton, St Budeaux Square and Victoria Road and all it's adjoining streets. All this water would cause the chapel to flood to a depth of about six feet which I witnessed several times.

Opposite the Fleetmoor Road junction was Westcott's coal yard where customers would place their orders . The Southern Railway would off load the coal into Westcott's yard where it would be bagged up into one hundredweight bags, put on a lorry and

dispatched to whoever had placed orders.

Moving up into St Budeaux Square, across the road from the Baptist Chapel, was H R Stancombe's who were a General Store, TSB the bank, a cafe, a butcher - first Cunninghams and later Reynolds, a wool shop, A E Mardons the newsagents, Stan's barbershop, Martins Dairy which sold all dairy produce, Uglows the bakery, Occleshaw's the tobacconist, the chemist and post office, an off-licence selling alcohol and spirits and the Trelawny which was a hotel and public house.

Opposite the Trelawny was a roundabout with a police box in the middle. To the right of this roundabout was the station shop which specialised in sweets and chocolates. This shop was the first shop that people disembarking from the stations came to. Also, opposite the Trelawny, was the road leading to Barn Barton and Saltash Passage. On the bridge between the Southern and Great Western Railways was a garage, known as Dyers Garage later run by Jack Williams, a short , plump man who was very jovial and who owned a red Daimler Roadster, which he was very proud of. He told me that there was only three made and he had seen the blue one and was on the lookout for the white one. In later years, he took me on as a part time taxi driver and as I got my petrol there, sometimes if I was a bit short of cash, I could get it on the slate.

Over the bridge, on the left, was a footpath leading to the rear entrance of Poole Park Road. This path also led you to Blackie Woods where my mates and I would sometimes spend all day. It was basically a natural adventure park. Also, immediately across the bridge on the left was Couches Fish and Chip shop and later the house at the junction of Barn Park Road, and the road leading to Saltash Passage, became the Bambino cafe. At the top of St Budeaux Square was the bottom of Victoria Road. A short distance up this road you would come to the State Cinema and this was a regular haunt. There were three performances every week. The first film of the week was on Monday, Tuesday and Wednesday . The second was on Thursday, Friday and Saturday and Sundays for one day only. It wasn't unusual for us to go to the flicks on Saturday, Sunday and Monday to see all the films, then that would leave the rest of the week clear to do other things. One Saturday night performance I always remember is that we were all standing in the queue waiting to go in and it suddenly became very noisy, George , the usher, and his word was the law, told us to quieten down to which one of our group replied, 'It's not us, George', and the noise continued. George promptly ushered our group out of the queue and told us that we were not coming in tonight, and somebody replied,

'That's alright, George, we'll go to the Forum in Devonport instead! We all made haste to the Square and caught the Number 6 Western National bus to Devonport. On our arrival at the Forum, we made our way up the steps and were met by the manager. Standing upright with arms folded he looked straight at us and said, 'I've been expecting you, you're not coming in here either!' . Somebody was wishing they hadn't told George where we were going. Don't you hate the telephone sometimes?

A steam train on its way to Saltash. In the background is the US Army Base at Vicarage Road. The house below the bridge, on the right, has an Anderson shelter in its garden.

Philip Syms remembered:
In St Budeaux, where the new St. Boniface Church now stands, was the old church hall . It was about 1947 when I joined the Wolf Cubs and their meetings were held every Friday evening. They were known as the 2nd St Budeaux troop. The 1st St Budeaux troop was at St Phillips which was in Bridwell Road (overlooking Weston Mill playing fields). In later years, a Scout group was started but unfortunately, there wasn't a great following so as an alternative a Sea Scout group was formed, with a better response. Beside the Ferry House Inn at Saltash Passage was a garage and this is where their boat was kept.

The staff of Easterbrooks, Victoria Road in 1948.
Included in this photo are a Miss O'Brien, Miss Backhouse, Miss Pike, Mrs. Avery, Miss Johns and Miss Thomas. Easterbrook's featured in the local paper on 12th August 1948:

Lorry Hits St Budeaux shop front

When Mr F R Easterbrook opened his shop in Victoria Road, St Budeaux, at 8am today, it was for the first time since the redecorations and alterations had been completed. Ten minutes later, he was surveying the wreckage of half of the front of the shop smashed by a lorry which swerved coming down the hill, mounted the wide pavement, and crashed into the shop.
The lorry also struck a stationary naval car, parked behind Mr

Easterbrook's own car, and pushed it up on the pavement. Fortunately, there was no-one on the pavement at the time, and none of the assistants in the shop were injured.
One girl, who was behind the counter, had to be sent home suffering from shock. The wooden counter was pushed back over two feet.

Mr Easterbrook was in his thirties at the time and a shop opened further up in West Park during the 60's and 70's called Easterbrook's. It seems very likely that this was indeed the same Mr Easterbrook.

More of the shop girls from Easterbrooks in 1948. This photo includes a Miss Scully, Miss Johns, Miss Williams and Miss Thomas.

Local children survey the damage to Easterbrook's shop in August 1948. This old newspaper cutting reveals the extensive damage and it's not hard to imaging Mr Easterbrook's displeasure after just having his shop refitted.

The 12th Plymouth Lifeboys based at St Budeaux on Church Parade along a street in Barne Barton. The Lifeboys were a junior Boy's Brigade within the Methodist church.

The early days of the St Budeaux Baptist Chapel. An old Morris Minor sits outside the building.

An early meeting outside the chapel. Unfortunately, although the photo still exists, there is no information to go with it. From the smiling faces, this looks like it could be a wedding group but if it is, the bride and bridegroom appear to be missing.

Here's a photo of the Boys Club. Some of these appear quite old for boys! They are shown mounting and displaying sea shells and bird feathers. On the wall, one of the drawn pictures features a man on a stretcher who has been knocked down by a lorry. Perhaps it was for a road safety campaign. Things have certainly changed since.

The St Budeaux Sunday School Teachers with Reverend Thomas.

Ten

The Tamar Bridge

The building of the Tamar Bridge brought much upheaval to the residents of St Budeaux. Below is a list from the 1950s of houses and properties that were to be compulsory purchased and removed to make way for the building of the bridge. Looking through the list, it's easy to see that many of these houses still remain today but it must have brought a great worry to their owners when the list was first released.

This notice informs land owners, lessees and occupiers of an application made to Parliament to empower Plymouth City Council and Cornwall County Council to either acquire or compulsory purchase the properties mentioned in the schedule, with regard to construction of a bridge across the River Tamar. Notices are to be sent to:
The British Transport Commission; The British Transport Commission (Western Area Board); The Lords Commissioners of the Admiralty (2); Mrs E M Harris, Ferndale, Saltash Passage, St Budeaux; Mr E J Trip, 884 Wolseley Road, St Budeaux; Mr L G

Hancock, Anemone Bungalow, Saltash Passage, St Budeaux; Mr E Burman, 2 Railway Cottages, Saltash Passage, St Budeaux; Mrs A Stewart, Ferndale, Saltash Passage, St Budeaux; Mr C Stoneman, 934 Wolseley Road, St Budeaux; Mr C E Hine, 57 Victoria Road, St Budeaux; Mr R L Stevens, Higher Ernesettle Farm, St Budeaux; HM Postmaster General, London; Mr R G Tubb, 1 Admiralty Road, St Budeaux; Mr A H Paice, 2 Admiralty Road, St Budeaux; Mr C E Bennett, 3 Admiralty Road, St Budeaux; Mrs R Richardson, 4 Admiralty Road, St Budeaux; Mr A F Toms, 5 Admiralty Road, St Budeaux; Mr C K Souster, 6 Admiralty Road, St Budeaux; Mr J L M Chavener, 7 Admiralty Road, St Budeaux; Mr E Large, 8 Admiralty Road, St Budeaux; Mr L G Comer, 9 Admiralty Road, St Budeaux; Mr C H Tavener, 10 Admiralty Road, St Budeaux; Mr A Pudner, 11 Admiralty Road, St Budeaux; Mr N B Hooper, 12 Admiralty Road, St Budeaux; Mr G W Johnson, 13 Admiralty Road, St Budeaux; Mr W A Oakley, 14 Admiralty Road, St Budeaux; Mr H C H Badge, 15 Admiralty Road, St Budeaux; Mr A A Samwell, 16 Admiralty Road, St Budeaux; Mr A L Burns, 17 Admiralty Road, St Budeaux; Mr A V Smithwaite, 18 Admiralty Road, St Budeaux; Mr C L Heath, 19 Admiralty Road, St Budeaux; Mr W T S Syms, Queen and Constitutional, James Street, Devonport; Mr A S Watts, 6 Newman Road, Old Walls, St Budeaux; Mrs B M and Mr R Stephens, 98 Normandy Way, St Budeaux; Mr F C Parsons, 1 Verna Place, St Budeaux; Mr B J Anstis, 138 Victoria Road, St Budeaux; Mr R E O Revell, 43 Waverley Road, St Budeaux; Mr W E Scull, 45 Waverley Road, St Budeaux; Mr R T Herpels, 28 Seacroft Road, St Budeaux; Mr G E Down, 20 Verna Road, St Budeaux; Mr S D Hassell, 65 Normandy Way, St Budeaux; Mr F Rundle, The Hall, 71 Normandy Way, St Budeaux; Cornwall River Board, Launceston.

I'm sure that many of the names mentioned in this list will be familiar to people living in the area close to the bridge. It's amazing that Ferndale, which stands right beneath the two bridges managed to survive the work. Nearby houses close to the Royal Albert Bridge Inn also survive as well as many others on this list.
A lot of people would have been dismayed at the building of the Tamar Bridge at the time but it's hard to imagine with so much traffic on the roads today, coping without it.
The Tamar Bridge was completed and opened in 1961.

This book contains just a few of the memories of people of St Budeaux. There are undoubtedly many, many more and it would be nice to record these at a later date before they are lost forever and people lose touch with what the area was once like and how it has changed in the past hundred years or so.

I hope that you've enjoyed reading this book and I hope that, if you're an older resident, it's brought back some fond memories of the past. I hope to capture more of people's memories in later books so future generations will be able to read and discover how St Budeaux has changed in recent history.

I have tried not to delve too much into the history of the area other than to include people's memories as much of this history is mentioned in detail in my St Budeaux and Saltash Passage books. I hope that it's proved just as enjoyable.

The Royal Albert Bridge Inn in the early 1900s.

98

By the same author :

St Budeaux

Derek Tait

St Budeaux

A history of St Budeaux, Plymouth. Contains over 150 old photos and illustrations.
108 pages.
Price : £9.99.
ISBN-13: 978-0955427763.

Saltash Passage

Derek Tait

Saltash Passage

A history of Saltash Passage, Plymouth. Contains over 140 old photos and illustrations.
104 pages.
Price : £9.99.
ISBN-13: 978-0955427732.

Plymouth Hoe
Derek Tait

Plymouth Hoe

A history of Plymouth Hoe. Contains 172 old photos and illustrations.
128 pages.
Price : £9.99.
ISBN : 978-0-9554277-7-0.

Plymouth
at War
Derek Tait

Plymouth at War

A history of Plymouth. Contains 200 old photos and illustrations.
130 pages.
Price : £9.99.
ISBN : 978-0955427787.

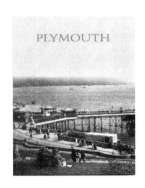

Plymouth

A history of Plymouth. Contains 200 old photos and illustrations.
130 pages.
Price : £9.99.
ISBN : 978-0955427794.

Saltash

A history of Saltash. Contains over 150 old photos and illustrations.
128 pages.
Price : £9.99.
ISBN : 978-0-9560781-0-0.

Mount Edgcumbe

A history of Mount Edgcumbe. Contains over 203 old photos and
illustrations.
172 pages.
Price : £9.99.
ISBN : 978-0-9560781-1-7.

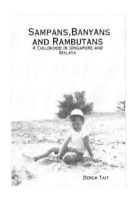

Sampans, Banyans and Rambutans
A Childhood in Singapore and Malaya

A childhood spent in Singapore and Malaya in the 1960s as part of a Naval family.
104 pages.
Price : £7.99.
ISBN-13: 978-0955427701.

Memories of Singapore and Malaya

Memories of Singapore and Malaya during the 1950s,1960s and 1970s through the eyes of servicemen and their families.
Contains 230 photos.
194 pages.
Price : £9.99.
ISBN-13: 978-0955427756.